The Sense of Love

Poems by Andrew M. Greeley

The Ashland Poetry Press
Ashland College
Ashland, Ohio

Printed in the United States of America

Library of Congress Catalog Card Number: 92-074851

ISBN 0-912592-33-8

For my classmates
from St. Angela Grammar School
Class of 1942
On our Golden anniversary

CONTENTS

EROS

PHILOS

AGAPE

Foreword

Wags like to say that Andrew Greeley has never had a thought that went unarticulated. Were this true, his diversity of disciplines and genres would give him a range seldom matched. An ordained priest since 1954, a professor of social science at the University of Chicago (from where he holds a Ph.D.), a researcher for the National Opinion Research Center at the University of Chicago, and a sought-after lecturer, he counts his books in three digits, and his essays and journalistic writings are nearly uncountable. He has in the past couple of decades become a best-selling novelist, writing, for want of a better term, romances (which have given him, in some circles, a certain notoriety), science fiction, and mysteries. Although or, perhaps, because his physiognomy is that of a leprechaun, he is often picked up by the news networks to comment on the likes of papal elections, birth control, and women in the church. His articulate, often satiric commentary on the hierarchy is legend. But many picking up this book may be startled that he is also a writer of poetry, another, and very different, medium for the articulation of his thoughts.

Until this volume, his poetry has to a large extent been privately circulated, which places him in the context of the priest poet of the Anglo/Roman tradition that includes John Donne, George Herbert, and Gerard Manley Hopkins, all of whom had only the amateur's audience--coteries of friends and family. The amateur (from the Latin *amator*) poet is indeed a lover of the possibilities of what can be made from words, their shapes, sounds, images, and the games for which they provide the playing field. In a sense, a *profession* of poetry writing has never really existed from Chaucer ("The Complaint of Chaucer to his Empty Purse") to poets of our day who live off the largess of university English departments. While the priesthood has sustained poets, at least since St. Patrick, there seem to be far more religious poets than poet priests.

There are elements, however, that seem to be peculiar to the priest poet. Certainly religious subject matter is important, but there have been priests who have written much poetry that is not on its surface religious poetry, as, for example, Jonathan Swift. There are those given to hymnody such as John Keble, who was an early leader in the Oxford Movement, and John Henry Newman, who progressed from that movement to Roman Catholicism, and a host of cleric "song" writers since Vatican II. The tradition includes John Skelton, who, like Greeley himself, is at the edge of priestly limits (as defined by bishops); the intensely pious English martyr Robert Southwell; the metaphysical Donne; the mystic Herbert; the satirist Swift; and the late Victorian and early modern Hopkins. It is interesting to note that these priest poets tended to flourish in times of religious upheaval. We find him or her posing questions that perhaps can only be answered by the pressure of the artistic use of language.

How does Andrew Greeley fit into the tradition? I find in this collection some parallels with Donne's use of the sexual metaphor of God's love, which has its basis with the Biblical image of the bridegroom of the soul. His "Holy Sonnet XIV" develops the conceit of the soul's being "betroth'd unto your enemie," so that unless God take him prisoner he can't be free, "Nor ever chaste, except you ravish mee." Greeley, in his novels as well as his poems, exploits sexual imagery to define the intensity of the love of God towards his human creation and the mystical return of that love. The sexual experience is perhaps the most powerful aspect of human sensibility outside of death, the ultimate human experience (which in Christian understanding means final unity with God), and death is, indeed, the most intense metaphor we have come up with for the sexual experience. Following in this poetic conceit (which St. John of the Cross also exploited), but in the argot of our age, Greeley gives us "Is God aroused for his human loves/With desire as fearsome as wedded want--/The hot humid hunger of a horny wife?"

Donne also felt the earth shake beneath him in terms of the "new Philosophy," science, which "calls all in doubt.../'Tis all in peeces, all coherence gone...." In our age, DNA can disturb the human spirit as much as did the new astronomy in the early seventeenth century, and Greeley in "Actual Graces: An Ode on Holy Saturday" confronts the staggering biological determinism presented by modern genetics.

At times we find that Greeley has the sensibilities of other baroque poets; for example, one might think of Herrick's joy in the natural world in Greeley's "Gamboling Gambles," where the poet follows a pair of Quails in his Thunderbird, delighting in their absurdity, and projecting the same pleasure onto a God who laughs in the same way at the absurdity of humanity. On occasion one finds the logical piety of a George Herbert (as in "The Cheshire God") and the satiric spirit of a Swift. In all Greeley is moved by his own age in the church, aware of preceding ages, and hopeful for succeeding times.

While the early modernist movement gave us no prominent priest poets, the revolution of Vatican II and the time just preceding it seem to have produced a few priests who felt the need to pressure language, among them Thomas Merton, whose modern mysticism is set, for the most part, in medieval monasticism that thrives in a century given to war by way of its co-existence and contrast. Raymond Roseliep, a poet of a modernist bent in his early work, turned in the last decade or so of his life to a mysticism that was closely allied to Zen but created haiku that marks our post-Vatican II spirituality--

> The Mass priest
> holds up bread
> the still point.

Daniel Berrigan is certainly post modern and grows out of the new church. His work is personal, passionate, witty, puckish, and somewhat eclectic in form, and it defines the pain of our century of war, confronting the moral questions of our time. All three share in the priest poet tradition, as does Greeley with this collection.

But placing any poet in a tradition implies, as T.S. Eliot tells us, an individual talent, and Greeley brings to his poetry an Irish wit that is tempered by Windy City politics, a steadfastness in his priestly calling through an era of priestly exodus, a piety that sees God's joke in creating the Grand Canyon, a Catholic liberalism that sees in the many facets of God the character of a teenager and celebrates the carnal symbolism in the Christmas tree that can "Charm open the timid virgin sky/ And seduce fecund sun and rain/ From her barren firmament..." but also sees through sham. He, most of all, has the modern lyrical ability to examine the self for what it is.

This collection is divided into three sections, titled with the three words that distinguish the sorts of love in the Greek: *eros*, the active love defined by the flesh; *philos*, the social love, manifested in politics, human relationships, ethnic identification, the world of nature, and human institutions; and *agape*, a spiritual love defined by faith, Platonic vision, nirvana, or many other definitions of the transcendental. One often hears the Greek language praised for having such a distinction as opposed to our single word, with all its ambiguity. Yet there are few poems in this book that couldn't appear under any of those three headings, which is, of course, what poetry is all about--the unity of sensibility, or, giving shape or form to diversity. In this case, a sense of love.

Robert McGovern
Ashland University
October, 1992

EROS

In Her Image

Written on the occasion of a symposium and art exhibit "In Her Image" at the University of California at Santa Barbara. The exhibit was entitled "Indian Goddesses and Medieval Madonnas.

I.

Such thin waisted athletes, these Hindu girls,
Too many arms, full bellies, softball breasts:
Erotic nightmare sirens who, it is said,
Reveal the earthly womanliness of God--
Tara, Kali, and those other lusty nymphs,
As sweet and friendly as a safety blitz,
Hard thighed, defenseless and battered on the ground.

Is God aroused for his human loves
With desire as fearsome as wedded want--
The hot humid hunger of a horny wife?

Culture bound ethnocentric, I prefer
The tender toughness of a teen-age Notre Dame,
Who, Brigid-like, does me in with a laughing smile.

II. (Inside the exhibit)

When these fleshy full-bodied women lived,
Their fertility scarcely contested death;
Their busy wombs and breasts were required
To out harvest mortality's deadly yield,
Their rich abundance a genetic ruse:

EROS

A miracle to reassure the timid tribe
That life-bearing forces would struggle on
So the fruit of womankind might survive.

(Outside the exhibit)

What, then, is this finespun, slim-hipped coed's task.
Her womanly wonders a cautious hint?
When fertile plenty becomes a dire threat
And womb and breast seem decorative at most?
Can she still flare a radiant sign of life,
A sun-bright sacrament of warmth and grace?

Jogger
Descendant of a primitive hunter-gatherer species

Gliding down the beach
Easily flowing grace
Thin shirt soaking wet
Strong, trim leg kicking up the sand
Hunter's body designed to run
Amid the tall savannah grass:

Your ancient mothers,
Some say, only gathered,
Left hunting to the males,
But why then running women
And so graceful in the morning light?

Women I've Met

Celibacy's pledge does not one sexless make
Nor purge a man from vivid fantasy;
A promise, mystery, for the kingdom's sake--
No harsh puritan but God's free servant,
Vulnerable to imagery and hormone,
Passions harnessed, perhaps, but, yes, still there:
Heart open to hurt and heal, less than stone,
Ready, spongelike, to sop up loving care.

No woman is mine and I belong to none,
Yet I'm shaped, refreshed and fashioned by their graces,
More than if possessed by only one,
Forced out of myself by their smiling faces--
No complaint, gracious Lord, much less regret;
By You enriched through the women I've met.

Visitor in a Bikini

Curled up in a chair

Small breasts
Soft white belly
Rounded haunches
Slender legs
All deviously deployed

Surprise treat

Like strong tea
With freshly bettered toast
And raspberry jam
In a cellophane package

From a safe distance

To be savored
And enjoyed.

Tomboy

She bats and runs and throws like one of the guys,
Holds her own in their yelling sandlot game,
Laughs when she wins (good loser, never cries),
Though a gentle baby-sitter just the same;
She hardly notes sly energies inside,
That ovular maelstrom in her tomboy verve:
Rock falling, rushing river, rising tide,
Subtle hint of a round, soft, teasing curve.

Thoughtless flower, time bomb set to explode,
Gentle slave of cosmic forces unasked,
The home-stealer will unfold a butterfly,
Lovely for nature's pleasant heavy task,
The tomboy lost: victim of life-creating drive?
Or wise androgyne hiding to survive?

Sisters

Irish crystal goblet twins, alloy strong,
Soft candle glow reflecting in rich white wine,
Gossamer grails, eye seizing, lingering long,
Shaped falsely fragile with hand bewitching line,
Swelling brooks of smoothly flowing cream
Ably wrapping the willing victim warm
To float, embraced, down the soothing stream,
Caught lightheaded in their barely hinted charm.

Subtle bodies, modest as misty rain,
Too demure to dare dream about unclothed,
Slipping unaware into blood and brain,
Timed tensely in sensual dreams to explode
As primal women inflaming with a touch--
Definitely, sweet sisters, you are too much!

Suzie at Forty

Not merely, graceful girl, genetic luck
Makes you now more lovely than long ago,
Nor, though it helped, tough, gritty Irish pluck.
Something deep down, a soft, shimmering glow....
Slender blackhaired vision, slightly wicked eye,
Trailing elegance like a subtle scent,
Quick laugh, warm heart, and sympathetic sigh,
Dazzling (unaware) husband, child, and friend.

Comic, pretty mirror of silver light
With cosmos charm in your tantalizing shape
Tells us the secret of endless youth on earth.

Be a flash of smile in our darkening night
(Only the reckless gamblers will end up safe):
We all must live as if yesterday were birth.

Complaint

On being trapped--willingly enough--at a summer dinner by three women with mostly unbuttoned blouses.
(For Gene Cooper)

Red-peppered sauce, barolo in the glass,
Lightly buttoned matrons, my senses are entranced.
Rounded charms, luring beneath sheer masks,
Distract like slave girls in a naked dance.

Vanilla ice cream clouds floating down the beach,
Their maternal shade inviting touch and taste.
So fresh and close, yet just beyond my reach,
Gut-twisted, pleasantly tormenting grace.

Not by accident your casual display
Of slender throat, smooth-skinned chest, bemusing lace.
Flaunting mystery and power, you play
Your game, seductive but discreetly chaste.

A line of low Irish hills at twilight,
A promise soft and magic in the mist
Of bittersweet, defying death's delight
From the many-colored lands in the west.

Permanent only in the human ape,
Under frail shoulders, surprise to attract
The uncertain male, so eager to escape,
Loving scheme of whoever planned the act.

EROS

Three docile toys, in Islam's paradise:
I'd fondle and caress you the whole day through,
But for life's Gracious Cause--She's on your side,
As on earth, doubtless I will work for you.

On Not Lamenting the Partial Eclipse of the Bikini by the Maillot

In song and story less is more.
On the beach this year more is less
As we observe along the shore
The art of womanly undress.

A second skin, a clinging wisp,
A coverage quite extensive, yet
Of woman not an inch is missed
(And even more's revealed when wet).

A few thin ounces quite enough;
Conventional, outrageous, free,
Proud but wingless sensuous seraphs,
Deep down they share the mystery.

Among science's great successes
Breaking mystery's subtle code--
By covering up, one undresses;
In hiding, great secrets are shown:

Nipples, convenience and delight,
Last year impossible to display,
Now, quite covered, they come to light--
Rounded smooth now démondé.

Under brown shoulders, supple, bare,
Their breasts they sharply actualize,
Controlled but free beneath the skies.
Notice, yes, but do not stare.

No moral issue will I probe
I simply note the symbolism odd
In dress (I am no xenophobe):
Our women tantalize like God.

Actual Graces: An Ode on Holy Saturday
Or, Through a Glass Darkly
(For Karl Rhaner, S.J.)

When new sex cells are manufactured in each generation, the winning genes are pulled apart and reassembled to manufacture new organisms...but the individual organism is only their vehicle, part of an elaborate device to preserve and spread them with the least possible biochemical perturbation. Samuel Butler's famous aphorism, that the chicken is only an egg's way of making another egg, has been modernized: the organism is only DNA's way of making more DNA. More to the point, the hypothalamus and limbic systems are engineered to perpetuate DNA.

--Edward O. Wilson,
Sociobiology: The New
Synthesis, *p. 3*

A person really discovers his true self in a genuine act of self-realization only if he risks himself radically for another. If he does this, he grasps unthematically...what we mean by God as the horizon, the guarantor and the radical depths of his love....

--Karl Rahner, Foundations of
Christian Faith, *p. 456*

The hypothalamic-limbic complex of a highly social species such as man 'knows' or more precisely it has been programmed to perform as if it knows, that its underlying genes will be proliferated maximally only if it orchestrates behavioral responses that bring into play an efficient mixture of personal survival, reproduction and altruism. Consequently the centers of the complex tax the conscious mind with ambivalence whenever the _organisms encounter stressful situations. Love joins hate; aggression, fear; expansiveness, withdrawal...in blends designed not to promote the happiness and survival of the individual but to favor the maximum transmission of the controlling genes._

--_Wilson_, op. cit., _p. 4_

Everything is grace.

--_Rahner_, op. cit., passim.

Imprisoned pawn, DNA doomed to serve,
Serf chained to evolutions's austere weight,
You are output, programmed by gland and nerve
In the computer-clicking genetic fate.
An anxious hypothalamus makes you hide,
Fortress the self against the thieves of life.
Reproductive genes drive you, scared, outside,
Where altruism confused your hapless plight.

Body curve, tender flesh, imploring thigh--
Species mechanism, screening in the fit,
Eager skin, exploring hand, surrendering sigh--
"Love" is but DNA's ingenious trick.
Endocrine excrete, synapses respond,
A physical reaction, quite commonplace,
Two reproducers in temporary bond,
Normal for the survival of the race.

Think your beloved unique...it does no harm.
Emotions neatly fit the computer's plot,
Functional for the species your partner's charm.
His (her) body chosen by assortive lot

For best distribution of egg and sperm.
Improving the human genetic pool,
A link between you, the limbus will confirm
To rear offspring before your passions cool.

Don't knock the scientific vision;
You are evolution's final primates,
Chromosomes blended by harsh decision
Of Selection's search for adaptive traits.
In genetic plans human love is small...
Still, unanswered questions, at least for some:
How come the gene? How come anything at all?
Or, to enter the thickest fog, How Come?

Sex, for most primates, is casual and neat,
Designed to fit life's orderly routine,
Quiet, unheeded save in time of heat.
Why then special love in the human gene
Before Homo Sapiens could emerge?
Prolonged embrace and passionate release--
How come this bond in blood's demanding surge?
Why for Humans a need which does not cease?

On Mystery's misty, magic mountain
Sustaining all in being, love impatient,
Conniving madly, makes the computer run,
Then hastens down as a secret agent--
Not like a decent God, distant and aloof,
But jumping through the hills, peeking in the windows,
Dancing in the garden, hiding on the roof
An ardent spouse, seeking his beloved!

EROS

Lover's tasty body, God's gifted spy,
Seductive trap, dragging self, unwilling, forth.
Refreshment luscious but the costs are high:
Undressed, to be toyed with, laughed at, made sport,
Then tossed aside, a rejected kitchen rag--
Radical risks the naked spirit daunt.
It turns, ashamed, lets blushing courage sag,
Wiped out, destroyed by a sniggering taunt.

But the spy is sacrament, aggressive grace.
Self tries to run, nerve-triggered hormones flow;
Pleading breast, pounding heart, appealing face,
Twist the chest, sting the eyes...then self lets go,
Defenseless now, unsexed by sex, possessed
Easily, yet surprised by a Gracious gift,
Taken by Her/Him with self oddly still obsessed.
God...lover...all is grace...and triumph swift!

Dazzling, the mirror power of the gene--
Schematic blinding love revealed through it,
His/Her more devious plot is darkly seen:
Heaven's nuptials by earthy grace are sealed!

Apparition

On the screen of black and white
A living-color face

Liquid spinning movement
Within a frozen frame

Quadraphonic laughter
After a single channel day

In a right-angled world
Your tri-dimensional shape

For my tundra mood
Your tropic hug

Despite my hopeless life
Your loving kiss.

PHILOS

For My Neighbors--Maggie, Rich, Nora, Patrick, Lally

A city set on a mountain top cannot be hidden.
--Matthew 5:14

In Chicago our God lurks everywhere--
In the elevated train's husky roar,
Beside the blinking lights of intensive care,
In the clamor of the soybean trading floor,
With those who suffer poverty and fright,
In the humid mist of summer by the lake,
On the Ryan through an icy winter night,
With a young widow weeping at a wake.

A city of beauty, hilarity, and pain,
Boundless energy and permanent unrest.
A terrifying, troubled, hopeful place--
Its challenges intricate and arcane,
Its opportunity...ah, the very best:
To be an unclouded light of love and grace!

Black-eyed Wife

A great man lies dying,
Gray, haggard, hollow.
But there is worse than death in this room
With its thick rugs and rich drapery;
Energies and forces fill the air,
Fearsome, primal, ancient
Spirits, good and evil,
With something terrible in between.

I don't like it,
This roar of heaven's wars,
My holy oils irrelevant,
My priestly words drowned out
By the din of spirits' battle.

Outside the peaceful lake, the routine traffic,
But here a struggle which was old when the galaxy was new.
In the next room friends' quiet conversation,
Here the sizzling electricity of good and evil,
Love and hate, order and chaos invisible.
Evil has come to conquer a good man's soul,
Chaos to reassert its fearsome hold,
Hatred to open its terrible abyss.

None of this for your local parish priest--
Against them my poor prayers are weak and vain.
I do not deal with demons and seraphim,
With psychic principalities and powers;
I only minister the Final Rites.

Through the demons that haunt this room
The black-eyed girl moves
With steady confidence;
She, young but as old as they,
knows them, understands their power,
A psychic lightening rod--
More a target, perhaps, than he.

They fight for two souls
In currents of dark and light,
The ordained powers of good
As always in retreat--
Don't count on me.

The black-eyed wife straightens the sheet,
Smoothes the spread,
Gently wipes his brow, Calmly takes his hand,
Softly repeats the prayers.
Her sensuous warmth routs the haunting chill,
The angels begin to hum
And mother church goes quietly to work.
The two mothers, church and wife,
Will not give up their son.

Tenderly the black-eyed girl
Yields her man to another,
Who someday must explain.

It is finished, the day is done,
The demons cackle, but they know they're lost;
The powers crackle, but their energies are spent.
Strange things are yet to happen.

PHILOS

No matter for the black-eyed woman--
She weeps but knows that she has won.

Outside the lake lies serene in the setting sun;
Mine was a minor role in that eerie play,
And I do not want another.
Irrelevant to the mighty contenders,
Priests with holy oil are common,
Indistinguishable--they come and go.

This night there was more at stake
Than I'll ever know.

Gamboling Gambles

Mr. and Ms. Gamble quail
Gambol down the road,
Pair-bounded ying and yang,
Hear my T-Bird, agree to panic.
She feints to the left,
He feints to the right;
Pendulum-like they sway back and forth,
Trying to escape their own arc,
Trapped in intractable terror.

As my T-Bird looms
They run faster, I drive slower:
He feints to the left,
She feints to the right--
I'm faint from laughing--
Yapping at one another,
Neither giving an inch
(Buyer and seller
In an Hasidic camera shop).
The T is upon them.
Straight down the road,
Like a Jack Nicklaus drive,
They compromise and fly away.

In my T-Bird shell, I laugh at them
As the lord God laughs at us.

Irish Light

I remembered that the men of this island had once gone forth, not with the torches of conquerors or destroyers, but as missionaries in the very midnight of the Dark Ages, like a multitude of moving candles, that were the light of the world.--G.K. Chesterton

(For Tom Cahalane on his Silver Jubilee)

From bog and hill and field the candles came
Bound for Fiesoli, Nairobi, Old Tucson--
Anywhere the light needed passing on.
Blithe spirits in the missionary game,
Bright pilgrims of the many colored land,
Erin's exiles everywhere at home,
Bursts of Celtic light under night's dark dome,
Servants of the Spirit and Her nimble plan:

Where you find the faith, likely too the brogue,
Wit and wisdom and just a hint of rogue
And hope and love to fill the human heart
As darkness retreats over yonder hill
At the news of the everlasting day,
And Irish sunlight reveals bright heaven's way.

Dublin

Some cities are male: my own,
Commodity broker not hog butcher of the world,
Still has broad Slavic shoulders
Beneath his carefully tailored jacket.

But Dublin surely is a woman,
Voluptuous matron in her middle years,
Demanding, attractive, repellent--
This city is Molly Bloom,

Wanton, faithful, prudish, enticing,
Weary, unlaced, experienced,
Quick to reject you, turn you off
And then cradle you in her arms.

Fitzwilliam prim, Ringsend raw,
Sandycove cold, Anna Livia dark
Gandon solemn, Grafton gypsy, Mountjoy mean,
Born in the Liberties, degree from T.C.D.

Asleep when you want to play,
Eager for frolic when you need rest,
Milanese fashions if it suits her whim--
Old clothes when you show her off.

In succession she is all her women:
Gore-Booth, Brigid of Kildare, Seanad,
Maude Gonne, Molly Malone, Delvacheem,
Kathleen Ni Houlihan, and always Mrs. Bloom.

Scruffy, vulgar, foul-odored, noisily obscene
Yet naked in the sun when rain is done,
Clean, sweet-scented, innocent--on her fair breast
A Medal to Mary, Mother of God.

Gray and dull and petulant, she dismisses you:
Your love is, thank you, not required;
Then, with a sunny smile, begs in sweet charity
That you come dance with her in Ireland.

Stay away from Dublin, I warn you all,
Beware her Georgian, Medieval, Celtic charm,
Her beguiling Irish laughter,
And rosary fingering Catholic faith:

She will torment, captivate, enthrall you--
Trapped by a Celtic woman, you'll be doomed
To feel her heat forever in your blood
And oft return to dance with her in Ireland.

Ballendrehid

(In memory of Canon McGarry, parish priest of Ballyhaunis,
County Mayo)

Grandpa walked down this winding track,
Left the white stone house where his life began,
Squared his thin shoulders, never once looked back,
The second son no one would see again.
The first-born stayed here, lucky, on the farm,
Wrestled life from this stern and soggy ground,
Enjoyed stone fences and home's familiar charm.
(An early death was all his brother found.)

His quiet, gentle offspring still work the land,
A task, but they are healthy folk and strong--
Their prospects here are not exactly grand,
Though, unneurotic, they know where they belong.
Sorry, cousins, I'm from beyond the sea:
Poor, sad grandpa; affluent, lucky me.

Ireland of the Welcomes
(For Ernie Evans)

"May you have a good trip," the old man said.
His smile, directions given, chased the rain.
Red-faced he tipped the cap on his silver head,
Softly prayed that God would bring me back again.
And the colleen small at an open door,
"Ah, sure, a bit you must eat and stay awhile."
They give all they have and something more,
Catch you in the warmth of an Irish smile.

If of Celtic charm you've had not enough,
Go to Glenbeigh road for music and the dance.
Welcomes flow as a stream in springtime flood--
Recall Paddy Reilly to Ballyjamesduff,
Hear a singing bishop, your final chance,
Can't stop, poor folk, it's in their Irish blood.

Kathleen Ni Houlihan

Cong County Mayo: Harvest Time

Young breasts restrained, model of elegance,
She pours the wine, alive as Galway glass,
High priestess of dubious opulence,
Serving the Yanks with what they think is class.
Yet one false move this haunted August day
And her robes will fall to the forest floor:
Wild fairy pipes will make our bodies sway,
Naked Eriu will lead the dance once more.

Here at Asford, quaint, peaceful charm for hire:
Quickly the hint of druid music dies;
Still we see signs of strange and secret fire
Flashing in her hooded and wary eyes.
Doomed to a time she does not understand,
She is Kathleen, this somber, captured land.

Sunrise from the Monte Mario
(For John Navone)

Smog broods over the sacred hills of Rome,
Dimming the city's pastel pink and white,
Hiding the tarnished northland-losing dome
From the early sun's purifying light.
In drab palaces heels click down the stairs;
Soon tiny cars will clog the ancient ways,
Making parking lots of quaint old squares
With churches placarded by PCI displays.

Passion unfulfilled but spent, they rise,
Old and new, from a couch of anxious lust
With mates they adore and yet despise,
Dreading to return at night, though knowing they must:
The Church, glum marriage broker, devoid of mirth,
Wrings its hands and grimly waits for birth.

At Bewley's Cafe

Ireland is the best country in the world to be a kid.

--Michael Hout

The blond doll, curly hair and all,
Is in fact an imp, a grinning little leprechaun.
Her young parents, when not devouring each other
With eyes of love, have joined her giddy game.

They laugh merrily at their clowning child
As, with pretense of mature delicacy,
She digs her fingers into the delightful icing
Of an intriguing sticky bun.

Aware that she is putting on a show,
Entertaining ma and da, she sniggers,
Smears each finger with gooey white
And then, one by one, licks them clean.

She beams proudly as, next to empty tea cups,
They lay their heads on the table,
And chortle helplessly at her wondrous act,
This shining partner in their fun.

Now it's time to go. Ma extends the coat
The imp puts her arms in the sleeves,
Wrong way round of course, so the coat
Must be zipped up in back.

With much struggling laughter
As the kid plays contortionist
They twist and turn
To get the coat on right.

She sees me laughing, I smile and wave.
She toddles over and grins up at me.
"A little monkey," her ma says proudly.
A gorgeous little monkey," I reply.

The parents beam, da pats me on the back.
They leave Bewley's serene
Someone else agrees that their kid
Is a very special little monkey.

After she has waved her goodbye,
I buy another chocolate for the road
And ask myself if I were made
For such play and fun by God!

A Conclave Sonnet

(For Grace Ann)

Our great glacier-melted lake turns most fair
When, troubled, it gropes for uncertain calm
Like a girl combing wet and tangled hair,
Rain swept and twisted by a manic storm.

Hair-line traced, fragile vase more lively made,
Lightly marked by steel-pointed sorrow's knife,
Ready still for flowers too long delayed
To grace subtle lines in the bloom of life.

Children do not mourn for the lost half day
When the noon sky lifts after summer rain
But praise the blue with an afternoon of mirth--
Hope broken, shattered, stomped on, then reborn:
First life lost, it was said, then found again--
Seeing death as the vespers of rebirth.

Summer Storm
(For Helen, after a visit in the hospital)

Sunbeams tiptoe over tumbling waves
And spray a pinpoint net of silver light
While the sky declines to hide in cloudy caves
But splashes color on the gray it fiercely fights.

Delicately spinning an eye-dazzling dance
On days like this, the foam turns purest white,
Surviving the lake's each crushing avalanche
And straining upward to seize a heaven's height.

When sickness tries to rip the mind apart
And drag the soul through the dank depths of night
In an elegant mix of faith and art,
Some will sop pain, ignite hope in their friends,
Giving strength to the would-be sympathetic heart
And trust that love sets tilted life aright.

Richard J. Daley (1902-1976)

Surprised, a great city hold its breath,
The harsh lake beats against an anguished shore,
Black headlines scream the news of sudden death:
Ink blot hero big as life--now no more.

Liberal vultures cackle on their high rise rocks:
Good riddance, no one will miss the boss.
But out in the neighborhoods ethnic folks
Both white and black, wonder and mourn their loss.

From Bridgeport, this quaint neighborhood, he came
And learned on these streets--Emerald, Halsted, Lowe--
Politics, the way the Irish play the game;
The story--not yet, maybe never told
How hold a city firm, as best one can,
In the ground with the cold corpse of a man.

For Nora Maeve

What liturgy, a feast of red and gold,
Mounts laughing incense from the burning leaves,
Makes joyful autumn don its vestments old
And wind hymn merrily in the waltzing trees?
Why do warm-hearted celebrants sing and dance
As their tired, snowdrift-dreading souls revive?
What festival causes such a happy trance?
Don't you know? Nora Maeve is five!

Though yet the spiteful blizzard winds will howl
As death's-head winter spews its bitter lies
And despair snarls a sharp-teethed frigid growl,
We see God's sparkling love in her ocean eyes,
Our faith till spring and life and love arrive--
Let us sing of hope: Nora Maeve is five.

Mary

Theological specialists cited the Pope's reference to Mary as a sign of his traditionalism. Progressive Catholics have avoided reference to Mary in recent years so as not to offend Protestants.--News Story

There is a correlation between strong images of Mary and sexual fulfillment in marriage and social commitment.--Research Finding

The broken Mary Myth cannot compete,
A loser in the symbolic marketplace,
Like the mighty dollar we've debased,
Turned tinsel-tattered in a slushy street.
Her iconology is obsolete,
Discarded as an ecumenical waste--
A worn-out image buried with all due haste
And quickly forgotten by a smug elite.

Yet sounds of happiness in the winter cold:
A young mother's joy shouted at the skies,
A young women's laugh chasing dreary pain.
Capricious, our universe will not stay closed,
Like the magic star Mary glows surprise,
And her hint that God is tender love remains.

Brigid's Day, 1985

Durable, gentle Bride, as alloy toughened steel,
Tender goddess of poetry, new life, and spring,
You still reveal God's creative energies
And still unshaken bring to the hearth Her love.
Surviving the leap from Old Faith to New,
Celt to Slav, Mick to Yank, your holy name
Once revered, then banned, finds honor new renewed
As teen-age "Brigies" celebrate your fame.

The first distant call of spring's flaming hope
On Inbolc's holy day, your feast and Mary's too,
We shivering Irish gather round to hail
Your delicious breasts, giving milk to all,
And renew our faith in God's alluring love
Through our sacrament, good Mary of the Gael.

The Fifth of May--1954
Ordination

The expected day was bitter cold,
Warning us perhaps
Of what we'd have to face--
But no hint of John
Or the unchanging changed
And the rock that came apart.

Would that our hearts were warm,
Ready for the frantic fray,
Light and quick, dancing in youthful glee--
But they gave us not the slightest hint;
Unprepared, we were standing docile there
When the roof came tumbling in.

A few escaped never to return,
Others ran for safe and quiet holes,
Still others stood mute, the end accepting.
Some, sensing fun, said let's begin to dance--
A blind leap long ago in the deeper dark.
Do it again? I've already told you so.

AGAPE

A Psalm of Protest at the Grand Canyon --Father's Day, 1979

(For Professor William McCready)

Hey, what I want to know is how come,
I mean, why did you build this place,
Whiping out seven different oceans
And a couple of mountain ranges too,
Baffling the experts as to precisely how you did it?

It's really too much, you know,
Too big, too wide, too deep, too everything.

So why this great big rainbow nutty hole in the earth,
This mad collection of antiquated and misshapen fruitcakes?
No respectable God would assume responsibility;
The Olympian athletes, for example, would think it
A tasteless, disorganized Dali-decorated rubbish heap.

Your servant Nancy (no one else's for sure)
Is reputed to have collapsed here
In hysterical laughter--an appropriate response.

An earlier clerical visitor (not one of *ours*)
Disapprovingly dubbed it nature's delirium--
Better theology would call it a monumental joke
From a deliriously comic God.

But for whom did you build this joke
(At least three million years ago)?

47

AGAPE

Archangels maybe...Michael, Raphael...that crowd?
They're big enough to enjoy it, certainly,
But unless I have been deceived they can't *see* it.

Giants sweeping in from outer space in hyper-drive chariots
For an occasional tour of our poor old Terra?
A lot of work for a few auslanders
Who should stay on their own planets anyhow?
Or maybe for *us*--
Smug Japanese and noisy Germans,
Old women hobbling on canes,
Young women bouncing in leotards,
Fat fighting children with fat fighting parents,
Sloppy poor white trash from Texas,
Arrogant affluent blacks in Chardin clothes,
New Yorkers pushing to sneak ahead of me,
Bitching in their noxious nasal whine,
Flirtatious three-year-olds looking for a papal hug--
Homo turisticus Americanus?

Noisy, vulgar, polluting, ecology destroying
Slobs whom the good environmentalists despise?

Maybe.

For it delights you to be with the children of men
Even when we're not all that delightful.
So perhaps it delights you to delight them
Monumentally, deliriously, and hang the Pepsi cans!

AGAPE

I know how daft you sometimes are.
You probably gouged this goofy gash in the ground
For the same reason you did the rest of the cosmos
(You should excuse the expression):
You did it for the pure, absolute, unmitigated
Unadulterated HELL OF IT!

A Creed of Metaphors

I. God the Teenager

That God exists in the world is not a proof
But a metaphor of who She really is,
An unrestrained adolescent, showing off,
An excessive, exuberant, playful whiz,
Determined gamester with the quantum odds,
An ingenious expert in higher math--
This frolicsome and comic dancing God
Is charming and just a little daft.

Will God grow up? Will She become mature?
In the creation game announce a lull,
Her befuddled suppliants assure
A cosmos that is quiet, safe, and dull?
Can God be innocent of romance?
NO WAY! On with the multi-cosmic dance!

II. The Pathos of God
After Rabbi Abraham Joshua Heschel

Like a geranium wilting in a drought
Or a weeping child lost in a crowded store
A lovely woman, alone, frightened, hurt,
Implores my sensitive and tender care.
I wipe away her tears and beg a smile;
I want to heal, to cherish, to ease her pain,
To gently say that in a little while
She'll laugh and love and begin her life again.

Is her pathos a sacrament of God,
Who, some say, weeps each time a baby cries?
Is the desire she stirs in me the barest hint
Of Her ultimate, astonishing surprise?
Can it be--O truly dazzling wonderment--
That God requires of me abandonment?

III. God the Romantic Lover
Love is forever but it does not last.--Brazilian parable

Paralyzed in a fragrant, languid bog,
Hostage to an incurable obsession,
Enveloped in a gentle rosy fog,
A willing victim of sweet infection,
I become a clown, a shameless naked slave
Bounced between ecstasy and dejection
A lunatic on a roller coaster wave,
A fool, innocent of all discretion.

"God is love"--is this what it really means?
Is God so heedless of my imperfections?
Captivated by daffy romantic dreams?
God, broken hearted by my rejection?
Like a love-sick and disappointed teen,
Does God hope love's death ends in resurrection?

IV. God the Homemaker

She who makes my home a habitat creates
Of concern amidst anonymity,
A center which affection animates
And order, love and magnanimity.
At home my soul and body she repairs--
Broken heart, running nose, and bloody knee.
She dispenses healing and restoring care
Not to an insensate number but to me.

The universe is not cold and dry
An absurd, infertile singularity
Beneath an empty loveless darkened dome.
God hovers over it with a lullaby,
And, bathing the cosmos with sweet charity,
She makes of it for each of us a home.

V. God the Storyteller

The pure, anguished notes of a Mahler horn
As they tumble round a mountain top,
Gossamer rainbow wings born on fragile breezes,
A hasty kiss I pray will never stop.

The front arrives with a cleansing gust of wind--
The hull tilts, sails flap; I duck the swinging boom.
The soggy gray clouds are gone, my soul revives
As ballooning spinnakers briskly tug for home.

A melody, changing wind, a quick embrace,
Metaphoric gifts that need not be but are
Mystery, wonder, marvel, amazing grace,
Seducing comic hints from the reservoir
Of eternal surprise, a tempting trace
For my dark night's journey--a newborn star.

VI. Lady Wisdom
Based on Audrey Hepburn as God in the film Always

When you wake up from surgery, a skillful nurse--
Compassionate, sensitive--a distant light,
A promise of peace and reassurance,
A loving mother to tuck you in at night.
No longer is there any need to hide,
All is seen and long ago remitted:
A sympathetic judge, a case already tried
And a verdict given--"you're acquitted!"

She's not a great accountant in the sky
Nor an old monsignor with a walking cane
Who wants to chase me quickly off to hell,
But a long-loved spouse who wipes away my pain
And draws me to her breasts that I may cry--
In her embrace things always turn out well.

VII. The Kingdom of God
The Kingdom of God is at Hand!

(For Leo Mahon)

Not a heaven's city of God, ivory and gold,
Nor a spired Byzantium here on earth,
A theocracy biblical and old,
Benignly ruled by goodly king and pious pope,
But a raging torrent, smashing through the ice
To rush in lethal flood madly towards the sea,
A firestorm that consumes and devastates,
A blood-red furnace spilling molten steel.

A dangerous demanding dynamism,
Yet somehow winsome--the famished divine
Desire unleashed, that is the kingdom of God!
The Creator's lustful fervor arisen,
A tumultuous, delicate hurricane--
The rapacious love of God falls upon the world!

VIII. A God Who Charms

After thinking in Hradcany Castle about Hapsburg religion forced for centuries on the people of Prague

Not by guidelines, rigid rules, nor canon law,
Nor by inquisitors and Hapsburg troops--
Tyrannies that trade a shaft for love--
Is the lonely human heart won for you,
But by a warm and mystic day in May,
With wild flowers dancing on the hillside,
As a band of friends eat a picnic meal,
And kids screaming on a circus ride--

A scoop of chip-laden chocolate ice cream,
Hope and faith at a noisy Irish wake,
The lover's body, a delicious dream
At sunset on a golden purple lake,
A pope who invites, bishops who smile and laugh:
For You are a church of charm instead of wrath.

IX. Irish Parent God
After watching Irish parents play with their children at a small
amusement park on the strand at Bray on a Sunday afternoon

Sweeping the laughing boy up with his arm,
Grinning and mounting the stairs of a giant slide,
He squeezes a tiny hand to bless from harm:
Father and son begin the gallant ride,
As mother and sister in spasms of giggles wait,
Munching on rich vanilla ice cream cones.
All four shout, ecstatically defying fate,
As two heroes plunge bravely to the ground.

You too are a doting parent who enjoys
The celebrations of Your girls and boys,
Who frolics with us at your play and toys
And protects us from what may destroy
Our innocent happiness and childish noise,
An Irish parent God who lives for our joy.

X. A God of Freedom
On Margit's Island* in the Danube near Budapest

Does an impassioned groom on his wedding day
Want to hear that his bride was given no choice?
Or, later, on the silver jubilee,
That her love was never given, always forced?
And, after a long quarrel is reconciled,
Does a rejoicing mother wish to learn
That richly renewed love and hope with her child
Was constrained and not by affection earned?

So why do pious folk like Bella Four
And parish directors of RCIA+
Try to force Your lovers to love their way?
Have You not said that all love must be free?
"Especially love between thou and Me"?

*King Bella IV of Hungary "gave" his newborn daughter to a Dominican convent on an island in the Danube in gratitude for his victory over the Mongols. Her fate was somewhat better than that of Iphengenia and she later insisted that she remained in the convent on her own volition. She is now known as St. Margit (Margaret) of Hungary and the island is named after Her.

+Rite of Christian Initiation for Adults. An anachronism created by liturgical theorists to reintroduce the old "catechumenate" from the ancient Church. "Catechumens are even dismissed after the homily, as they were fifteen hundred years ago to protect the "Discipline of the Secret" from spies in the pay of the Roman Empire that expired long ago. In many parishes it has become a pretext for rigid ideological indoctrination of those who wish to join the Household of the Faith.

XI. The God of the Parables

An indulgence no parent could defend--
Warm welcome to a fawning, worthless son;
A day's pay for those mumbling at the end
From a silly farmer when day's work is done;
A woman whose sins all right minds offend,
Her forgiveness from the judge quickly won;
A broken man whom no one will befriend
Finds himself redeemed by a Samaritan.

O God of Jesus, you're quite around the bend,
Not to be outdone by human folly.
What sort of crazy message do You intend?
By what madness do You propose to stun?
"You cannot comprehend the big surprise?
The triumph of My love has just begun!"

XII. The God Who Died
On Good Friday Love went where it had never gone before.

--John Shea

Soon will I leave on that dreadful pilgrimage
To travel fearfully I know not where,
As from my precious life I must disengage...
Yet, Love, have You not been already there?
A reassuring friend when I embark,
A tender guide across an unknown land,
A fellow traveler in the lonely dark,
A Beatrice who gently holds my hand.

For are You not the God who chose to die?
Is that not what Your Kingdom finally means?
That You right next to me will lie,
And death is not ultimate as it seems?
Both born again, You and I, from life's womb,
Will together leave behind an empty tomb.

Lynnie

God-like
I made you
Out of dreamy stuff--

Apricot figment--

Human-like
You struggle free,
Lusting for life
Of your own

Revealing me

God-like
I now
Belong to you.

A Novena for the End of March

Palm Sunday
The Child waved her palm
Saving it from the dirty slush
Herself Hosanna

Naked City
Spring came suddenly
And embarrassed the city
Without her green robe

Kids on the Street
Freed from winter's jail
Kids tumble outdoors, their shouts
Ripping the soft air

Lake Michigan
Frosty cloak shrugged off
The lake, over supple shoulders,
Slips on a new gown

Rumpled Sheets
Long snow blind, naked
Spouses in Sunday sunlight glow
See their love again

Magnificent Mile
Wild coltish south wind
Gamboled madly down the street
Peering under skirts

AGAPE

Water Tower place
Women's deft bodies
Straining against light spring dresses
Gracefully hint hope

Blessing the Font
Sunlight melts the ice
May renewed risen Jesus fire
Flame our sterile lives

Paschal Pieta
With her springtime smile
In gentle and warming hands
Mary holds the world

Summer Dream
(For John and Ann Marie)

Summers were hotter then, it seems to me.
Courting couples walked arm-linked down my street,
Sure that the Depression would always be.
Stockyard smell at night...How I loved the heat!
I dreamed often of a house by the lake
And caressing waters in the sunset glow.
Then cruel, wrenching waves through the windows break,
Clutching, dragging all happiness below.

And I still yearn for humid summer days
And revel in each thick and steamy night,
In dreams still see the harsh, shattering wave
Crashing towards the house, blotting out the light.
I'm not sure why but things have oddly changed:
Now the waves fall back and the house remains.

Dancing God and Friend
(For Mrs. "Church" upon her return from the hospital)

God, insidious neighbor, lives down the street,
Scheming and plotting a devious romance,
Starting the music, pounding out a beat,
Inviting all of us: "Hey, come to my dance!"
Shrewd, he gets us first by moving our feet--
A wild raucous God, grabbing every chance,
Reveling in noise, turning up the heat,
Catching our bodies in a foot-stomping trance....

Swaying at the door, a hand-clapping dame,
Fun poking fear, crazy voice-making din,
Shouting out orders. You're playing his game,
First at the party, dragging the rest of us in,
Spinning us round, making us dance all night
To the madcap rhythms of the Lord of Light.

Aria for the Christmas Tree

Axis Mundi,
Soaring cosmic center,
Erect ladder teasing heaven
So ardent, carnal earth can
Charm open the timid virgin sky,
And seduce fecund sun and rain
From her barren firmament,
Rorate caeli desuper
Et nubes pluant Justum;
Always verdant tannenbaum,
Evergreen in negligee of snow,
Spring's diffident allure promised
In the winter solstice night;
Christ's fiery cross
Piercing heaven's gate
Inundating all creation
With a tidal wave of grace;
Angel roost,
Lux in tenebris,
Circled by love's gifts,
Bearing the first fruits
Of God's torrid hunger:
All of us who are reborn
In Bethlehem.

Christmas Candle

Pledge of spring in the winter night,
May blossom in a field sealed with snow,
Touch of exploding fury
In which the universe began,
Promise of passionate, raging love
In triumphant possession turned tender
Seed of life melting solid ice
And making fruitful frigid water,
Healing hint of summer sun
Teasing greenery from barren earth,
Reconciliation triggered, love renewed
Gloom shattered on the journey home.

The Light came into the darkness
And the darkness could not put it out.

Wipeout
(For the Brennans--friends in need)

Skilled ballerina, spinning on the spray,
She slices through the wake with disdainful ease--
A mature woman, elegant at play,
Aloof, discreet in her capacity to please--
Then the tizzy teen-age trickster topples from her skis,
Cartwheels through the air, dancing on her face:
A carnival comic choreography,
A somersaulting epiphany of grace.

Devised by God to guarantee the race,
Who gifted them with smiles to incandesce the day,
Sculpted summer sunbursts to celebrate in space
And with sunburst color splash our humdrum gray
A designer impeccable in taste
Such sacraments crafted to delight us on our way.

Delvacheem

*Old Irish. "Fair Breast." The heroine of the Legend of Art MacConn,
and Irish version of the Quest for the Holy Grail. Both the Grail and the
Girl are sacred vessels representing God. Unlike Lancelot, Art MacConn
manages to bring home both vessels.*

Symbol of God, are you, girl, saving grace--
Her warmth in your fair breast's inviting glow?
Fire and ice, revealed in your soft embrace,
Black hair on white shoulders, lava on the snow?
Does She arouse, inflame with timid eye,
Respond, pliant, meek to our hungry need?
Give Herself in love with complacent sigh,
Seek our pleasure with single-minded greed?

Then ravished, does She turn us fugitive,
Hunting with now enraptured charms?
Caught by Her, wildly, madly, pinned captive,
Imprisoned in forever loving arms:
Thus Her feather touch sets our hearts awhirl--
It's You we see in the body of this girl.

Echoes

Tinkling cattle bells
Called down the candy clouds
So I could walk the hills
Along a singing forest road
To the marble city wall
By a large and quiet lake.
A beach ball, ten feet high,
Colored like a loony rainbow
Chased me to the shore.
Agfa colored sails lightly stirred
As the ships rocked gently
Near the castle lawn.
Pink straps confined
Pale white shoulders
And tender ivory throat
Framed in satin blond
And velvet Haydn strings.
The great jack pine
Stood astride the path
Reaching to the stars.
Wild cactus plants
Exploded like apaches
And swarmed upon the town.
A hand reached out
Split the darkness open
Offering a tad of light
Illumined cold brown hills
Rumbled out the fog
And chased away the night.

AGAPE

Flower blossom tang
And sweet soprano songs
Routed me out of bed
Into the raging storm.
Silver olive branches
Bent lightly in the breeze
And snow white window panes
Green surf foaming bubbles
Teased champagne bellies
Touched skim milk bosoms
Eager on the strand.
Sullenly the sun went home
In a flaming snit
So envious of the moon.
A stained glass afterglow
Hints of flaming passion
Soaking the bloodied sky
Anxious coyote laughs
On the shadowed desert floor
Scorpions crawl slowly home
And the puma prowls the ruined walls
Searching for his brief encountered mate.
One by one the window lighted hills
Blink discreetly out
Screen lovers quick falling veils
And deftly merging needs
While aimless ghosts glide by
With their hint of fearsome death.
Sparkling like Wisconsin lakes
Laughing blue eyes
Tear apart the gloom.

Clown grinning little girl
Spins her giddy swing
To sky and back
While her cowboy brother
Plunged down the slippery slide
And in the splashing lake.
The fine salt-laced air
Savored of strong red wine
In a slender chalice.
Mint flavored ice tea
As clean-earth rain
Soaking thirsty sands
Licked hot and weary skin
In the cemetery silence.
Soft footfalls, uncanny words
The dark shapes cringed
Under quickly scudding clouds.
A drag and dusty day
Harried by darting demons
Turned sweet in tasting
Raspberry delicious lips
Drained thick-whipped cream
At lavender languid dawn
From flowing fountains
Of chocolate malted breasts.
Heels clicking on concrete walks
Stabbed the quiet spring
And urged the trees to bloom
In distant humid August
Hard running thighs crash
Against lace light curtains
And thunderheaded noon.

AGAPE

A haze of golden smoke
Bathes burgundy quiet ponds
Tinged with silken silver
And barbecue tainted mists.
A zither mocking Bach
Dancing behind the scenes--
Mozart on the run.
Voices floated in the wind
Chiming on the thin night glow
Inviting all to come.
Captured by lilac light,
Modest in citrus scent
And half a light blue slip
Discreetly sipping moonbeams.

The Cheshire God

A wisp of cloud clinging to the mountain peak,
A tumbleweed roaming the desert sand,
Our cheshire God lurks everywhere we seek,
Slipping away just as we extend our hand.
His news he tells us and quickly, then, departs:
His design is to tease us and perplex,
Most effectively in the stirring of our hearts
The other self revealing in the other sex.

In raw hunger the mind and body seize
A love changing as the months and seasons run;
It ebbs and flows in the liquid fantasies;
There are not twelve others, only one:
Our dark mirror of unfathomed mysteries,
As scary as the night, bright as morning sun.

Marilyn

A still life in my memory, aflame
As a Van Gogh blossom, radiantly fresh,
Unfaded by the claims of age and pain
Or the first quiet hints of lurking death.
Girl and woman in delicate suspension,
Deft painting bathed in a blue and golden glow--
Perfection, promise in one dimension
And a self that has only begun to show.

Wife, mother, widow, forty years have fled,
Does your story, just begun, approach its end?
Are your bright grace and promise already dead?
Hope remains, distant rival, do not bend--
You were not misled, at fourteen, by god's love:
We shall be young once more, we shall laugh again!

Christmas Carols, After the "O" Antiphons

Based on symbols from the Jewish scriptures and sung at vespers the week before Christmas

O Wisdom

You come forth from the mouth of the most high and reaching from beginning to end, you ordered all things mightily and sweetly; come and teach us the way of prudence--December 17

Agonized engines in frustration moan,
Spinning tires strain against the frozen slush,
Caught in a cosmic traffic jam, each alone,
While the universe reverts to primal mush.
Life a brutal mess wreathed in tailpipe gas,
Emptiness crudely packaged by random change,
Our kind, trapped in a blizzard, a struggling mass,
Blinded while angry snowflakes madly dance.

In the distance through the swirling mist
A warming glow, an incandescent window pane
Where laughing tender grace may still exist--
Ending with a single touch confusion's reign,
We glimpse through the dense snowdrifts in chaos
To soothing love's brief flare, some hint of sense.

O Adonai

...and Ruler of the house of Israel, You appeared to Moses in the fire of the burning bush and on Mount Sinai gave him your law. Come and with an outstretched arm redeem us.--December 18

Seductive lover, O December cold,
Caressing subtly with your lovely hand
Twining around my weary, battered body,
Promising peace in your icy wonderland:
"There is no warmth, no reason to struggle more;
Drink deep from pleasure in my skilled embrace;
Retreat from your pathetic pointless war;
Come to me, relax amid my snowy lace."

Your erotic charms draw my clutching hands,
Yet the unconsuming mountain love still flames
(Cruel lover, refusing my frightened no).
Another mistress, fierce in her demands,
Implacable, uncomforting her claims,
Drags me onward, harshly through the snow.

O Root of Jesse

*You stand for an ensign of humankind; before You kings shall keep
silence, and to You all nations shall have recourse. Come and save us,
and do not delay.--December 19*

Trinket laden limbs, grasping for the sky,
Hollow symbol raised for a plastic feast,
Rootless, withering, turning brown and dry,
Tarnished star for magi from a witless east:
Harmless forest of gaudy tinseled trees,
Lighting every lawn against the winter gloom--
No more the Center, strong in the frigid breeze,
Axis Mundi, earth's lust for heaven's womb.

Yet look quickly, after your Christmas wine,
Each glittering tree has become a cross:
We--the branches, the world's light, the vine
Changing death to bright gain from senseless loss
Before it fades in after-supper strife--
Climb, like fabled Jack, the tree of life.

O Key of David

...and scepter of the house of Israel: You open and no man closes, You close and no man opens. Come and deliver him from the chains of prison who sits in the darkness and shadows of death--December 20

Sinus-clogged, jet-fatigued and motion-sick,
Our cell begins to shrink; the air grows thin;
Slowing down, wearing out, and giving in,
We sense the body's swiftly burning wick.
Slaves to gene, habit, sex, and social class,
Seeking all, we accomplish nothing much:
Durable as fragile blades of grass
Born to quickly die--a bit of cosmic fluff.

Chain-gang pilgrims slouching down the road--
Bent low under the whips of fear and hate
(No turning key to flood our jail with light):
Each year more failures in our heavy load,
No one to break the chain, transform our fate,,,
Hush, be still...freedom comes this Christmas night.

O Rising Sun
*Radiance of the light eternal and Sun of Justice; come and lighten those
who sit in the darkness and the shadow of death--December 21*

Spirit drawn tense, pulled, snapped broken at last,
Lost tempers while the noisy bells still ring,
Manic drunken carolers loudly sing,
Tattered tinsel memoirs from the bitter past.
Kill the pain before the start of midnight mass,
Rejoice in haste at the coming of the King,
Then let this hectic winter solstice fling
And quickly turn to the sullen family bash.

Ah, January, my body can start to mend.
Amidst the frozen stillness of winter's night,
My soul turns sick with germs of chilling doubt.
One less Christmas before my final end,
Yet each dark day yields a sliver more of light
And the blackness will never put it out.

O King of Nations

...and the desired one of all, You are the cornerstone that binds two into one.   Come and save poor man, whom you fashioned out of clay-- December 22

Naked to your love, stranger, I flee ashamed--
What I really am you must not see;
In your embrace, the self, helpless and inflamed,
Given to you, there's nothing let for me.
Depthless terror in your sweet affection,
I do not want you at my Christmas board:
You must die, fearful love, before I eat,
With a heedless word, or, brave man, with sword.

Dread diversity, joke of a drunken God
Splashing color sloppily, size and shape;
Seen briefly in the blazing solstice sun:
Creation variegate, Christmas present odd,
I'm held, terror land delight--no escape
From graceful love, the risk of two in one.

O Emmanuel
...our king and lawgiver, the expected of the nations and their savior, come and save us, O Lord our God--December 23

Life's treats from an upended stocking pour,
Deluging me beneath the magic tree,
Thick and rich with candy; yet I want more.
Soul weighted, despite the loud festivity--
Stomach stretched, limbs heavy, spirit sad:
Full yet empty, sated not satisfied.
Life's feast, clad in mourning, slips away,
Pursued by terror; something died today.

Joyous wrapping paper torn, tossed aside
To burn tomorrow in my private hell....
Dim song, faint music stirs the wind outside:
"He has pitched his tent, among us to dwell:
The one we seek, for whom all hearts have cried
Rejoice, Rejoice! He comes, Emmanuel!"